FREEDOM FROM CONFORMITY

FREEDOM FROM CONFORMITY

◆

PART II

MM JED

iUniverse, Inc.
New York Lincoln Shanghai

FREEDOM FROM CONFORMITY
PART II

iUniverse books may be ordered through booksellers or by contacting:

iUniverse
2021 Pine Lake Road, Suite 100
Lincoln, NE 68512
www.iuniverse.com
1-800-Authors (1-800-288-4677)

ISBN-13: 978-0-595-38464-8 (pbk)
ISBN-13: 978-0-595-82845-6 (ebk)
ISBN-10: 0-595-38464-1 (pbk)
ISBN-10: 0-595-82845-0 (ebk)

Printed in the United States of America

Contents

INTRODUCTION

This book is part two of a two part series and the reading of part one FREEDOM FROM CONFORMITY, SOCIAL & RELIGIOUS is recommended in conjunction to reading part two. Part one enhances the reader's awareness in understanding the fundamental nature of this book and challenges the reader to take a more serious approach to recognizing and understanding the beliefs that social and religious organizations attempt to impose upon us.

Every person who reads this book will interpret the subject matter differently. Each will translated the meaning of the words based on their past education, experiences and religious beliefs. Some may not hear or identify with the intended message. A conditioned mind can subtly distort and change the original theme, frequently without the knowledge of the reader.

Often times we "think" we see everything clearly but usually we are just looking at the superficial with the influence of what others have told us. Our belief system is based on fear, thinking about ourselves with the desire for power, position and self preservation.

Inwardly we are demanding that everyone believes as we do because we feel safe if no one opposes our view point. Unfortunately we will never understand and see the vast intricate interchange of life when we malfunction with a closed mind, when we hide in a theological box. The insecure carnal man feels comfortable and safe in its own special interest groups but our true inner man wants to be receptive and see the whole of reality not just a partial piece of it.

None of us wants to walk in deception not even at a small degree. However in order for us to comprehend reality we must experience awareness without condemnation or justification obscuring our thinking. Forcing our minds to think a certain way or to be totally blank will only result in blindness. Only a mind that is quiet and open will be able to observe everything without any confusion.

Our old selfish character needs to cease with all its opinions and judgment to the point that "self" becomes non existent. When this passive awareness occurs true peace and tranquility ensues. Sadly there are many who are still entrenched in their petty little lives that their ego will not allow them to even consider such an understanding. They think they are happy in their present condition and feel it would be foolish to make any sacrifices, there is nothing to gain.

Can we human beings solve the many issues that seem to be plaguing the world? If we are the cause of most of the problems how can we solve them. When our thoughts are always about protecting ourselves and self perpetuation is it even possible to stop the destructive direction society is taking.

Let us together take a closer look at leaving behind the old self-centered man and venture into that which is eternal, timeless and immeasurable. At first glance this writing will appear to be "undermining" the beliefs you have in God or the things of the spirit, in some ways that is true. To be more accurate, it is about clearing away all the counterfeit ideas that man has created over eons of time and then taking up residence in a new deeper level of awareness.

If you have never been given the opportunity to read and consider such a message of freedom as what you will read in this book, be careful, you will need to consider it with an extremely sincere and uninhibited mind. You may need to read it slowly and over and over again just to see past your programmed thinking. I do not say that out of arrogance because each and everyone of us can see and comprehend the truth equally, nonetheless all humans have a problematical issue seeing outside their current ideology. To look beyond our existing belief system with an unbound and receptive spirit is almost impossible.

I encourage you to look past your initial analysis of what you think the general theme of this book is about. Proceed with an open mind and give the words permission to speak to you, you will soon realize the message contained in this book is precisely what your inner being is yearning to manifest.

Some readers will simply not like this book or any book that challenges them to look beyond themselves. None the less a neat thing happens when anyone reads and hears the words of life, seeds of truth are planted deep into their timeless being that will someday sprout into reality.

Keep in mind that my goal is not to give you a system or formula for success. Each of us alone must recognize the truth and allow it to become alive in our inner being. However I would like to present to you some questions that you may ask yourself as your journey of enlightenment becomes an eternal presence. These questions are for the purpose of understanding our intimate motives so that our thoughts and actions may not lead to self destruction. This journey is not for the faint hearted, in fact if we are not extremely earnest in leaving behind our narcissistic desires it will be impossible to comprehend reality.

Part 1
UNDERSTANDING COMES WHEN WE SEEK NOTHING

We think that we are great thinkers, we think that we understand everything in our lives clearly and directly. Do you know that often times we are deceiving ourselves because of our own searching and seeking. Therefore the first question we need to ask ourselves and understand is what motivates us.

A fundamental and constant desire many people feel is to "be something" in this world of competition. We feel it brings us security. Unfortunately most people believe that the same is true in their next life and go to extreme measures to earn their right of passage and entry into paradise. We will look into this issue of earning our eternal salvation later.

The instant there is the craving to become something or to attain something, we are mislead. This is a very challenging deception for anyone to recognize and be free from especially for young adults as they enter the rivalry of society.

My wife and I are extremely blessed with five wonderful children. As I write this book our three oldest kids are in college, Arizona State, Iowa State and Augsburg College in Minnesota. The two youngest are planning on attending a college of their choice in the near future.

Just like most of us they have set goals that they would like to achieve. Hopefully they will not become obsessed with their goals and motivated by fear, greed and discontentment, instead we hope they will value and give their best effort to the present moment that they are living right now. Following is a poem (by an unknown author) that was included in my high school year book, I sometimes read it to remind myself to simply enjoy where I am.

Live every moment as it comes;
Take what it brings to you;
Be happy with the things you have
Each day your whole life through.

Take every step one at a time

And make the most of it…
Then, looking back, don't wish that you
Could change it a bit.

Make every hour that you spend
Mean just a little more,
So all the ones that lie ahead
Will be worth waiting for.

And don't put off those "little things"
Try to fit them in somehow,
For the time when you'll enjoy them most
Is not "someday" but now!

Isn't that a encouraging poem about living every moment as it offers itself to us. This poem also reminds me regarding the peer pressure that kids are dragged into as they grow up. Frequently the parents are those that influence their children the most to conform to the greed of society. We think that as we age we grow out of these childish ambitions to be equal or better, but in reality the demands of society intensify into an even stronger "adult peer pressure".

Malcolm S. Forbes once wrote that "the purpose for education is to replace an empty mind with an open mind", sadly that is not what usually occurs. The goals and ambitions of many young adults once they graduate from high school or college is to become wealthy and retire to a life of leisure. Everywhere we look there is someone preaching or selling a scheme to "get rich quick". Their purpose is seldom about living a full and happy life by helping others but rather seeking self amusement at any cost even if it harms others and damages the environment. Their whole mission in life is to "out do" their neighbors in obtaining worldly riches so they can obtain the newest toys on the market. They feel especially superior and arrogant if they can acquire a new thingamajig before everyone else.

Through lack of knowledge we believe worldly wealth and pleasures will take away all our fears and anxiety and bring lasting joy, but instead our acts of egotism and disrespect for others only produce the opposite, conflict and pain in every aspect of our lives.

If you are beyond your childhood years and your upbringing was pleasant you will probably remember trying to go back home and experience again your "feelings of youth'. You remember the good old times when the pressures of life seemed nonexistent, where you found total peace by simply playing a game, counting the stars or building a snowman. Have you noticed that if you try going back in time it is never the same, everything is different including you.

Children want to jump ahead in time to obtain their hopes and dreams while older folks want to go back to when everything was innocent and free. Time travel is not a means to happiness, reality is living in the present moment, whenever it is. Albert Schweitzer wrote "Truth has no special time of its own. Its hour is now—always". We will look at the illusion of time further in part two.

I would like to encourage you to examine your motives each and every time you feel the desire to obtain something, dispose of something, or in other words to change something. Ask yourself, do I want or don't want this simply because I am comparing it to what others have or don't have. Do I want or don't want this because someone told me that I should. Do I want or don't want this because I'm thinking about yesterday or worried about tomorrow and not living in the "now". Do I want to be somewhere else. Ask yourself if your desire is based on fear. True freedom is freedom from the mistaken feeling that you lack something. Let's insert a book mark here that we may come back and reference this paragraph later.

** BOOK MARK **

"Life and reality is only now", keep this thought at the forefront of your attention, secure it around your neck as a constant reminder just like you would a necklace. Never take it off, let it become entrenched in your every thought. Time cannot be used to fix anything. Whatever happened one second ago is old and what is going to happen in the future is not reality yet. Can you exist in that divine place where you don't try to change anything? When we do not desire anything, not an answer, not a explanation, not a solution, not any type of security, only then can we see with the eyes of faith.

This attribute of ultimate faith is a mystery to the narrow minded, it cannot be observed or experienced by a mind dominated with fear. They cannot begin to understand why an enlightened being is not struggling to alter or modify anything. When we get upset or lose our temper it reveals how weak and insecure we are. The more we react and try to change the circumstances around us, the further it provides evidence of our selfishness.

Our selfish desires create our greatest troubles, we are always seeking a result for ourselves. We talk about brotherhood but deep down it's our self-centered goals that put us against each other. We think that our beliefs (personal, social & religious) help bring unity but it is just the opposite, it divides us.

Frequently we are more concerned with our ideology than we are about solving the real issues. This is particularly true with a religious or political psyche. The religious or political mind identifies with a specific belief, with a specific method that will bring pleasure, security and rewards. They are held hostage by their beliefs and are powerless to see the whole picture, blind to recognizing the truth.

The numerous occurrences from our past that we remember and hold on to have become a huge influence on how we react to everything. We are talking about living by memory which is old. If we approach a problem based only on our past knowledge, we force our point of view based on our past experiences and we operate with tunnel vision.

Have you ever bought something that came with instructions to assemble and you ignored them thinking that you knew how to put it together. If you have and it included numerous pieces and it was difficult to assemble, you probably needed to stop and read the instructions. On the same note, the different roads each one of us must individually travel throughout our lives can be better navigated when we are willing to listen. Understanding comes when we are quiet, with an open and free spirit.

Part 2
COMPREHENDING THE TIMELESS

The splendor that we can experience along our journey is not based in the realm of time. This grandeur of the timeless is recognized when we understand the structure of time. It is impossible to use time as a means to understand the timeless. We are not talking about hours, days and years, it would be silly to throw away chronological time, we would be late for supper. Instead we are talking about not resisting the present because we are observing through the eyes of our past. If you stop for a moment and look closely at your inner thoughts, you will see that they are the result of all your yesterdays.

To often the "present" is used as a bridge to travel from the past to the future. We always want to be something different, do something different or be somewhere else. What usually happens is we remember our past experiences that were satisfying and we yearn for them to continue or we desire to go back to them. Or there are the negative memories which we seem to never get free from or forgive someone if needed. Do you catch yourself feeling remorseful about something you should or should not have done in the past. Do you or others around you spend lots of time and energy talking about the past? The damaging thing about living in the past is that we miss all the beauty and energy of living in the present moment.

So time is manipulated by our constant desire to change "what is". Many people believe that time is essential for transformation. They frequently feel that "I am this way but I want to be something different". We remain in our present condition during "time travel" therefore our goals are never achieved. If we use time as a method to obtain a quality or state of being, we are overlooking "what is really happening now".

Sometimes we try to make a change in our lives by practicing new actions but the practicing itself demonstrates that we are still living in the old circumstances and a true change has not yet taken place. If the change already took place we would not need to rehearse to prepare for the future. Rather it is a peaceful and tranquil spirit that produces transformation. This is why our happiness is not a product of time, real satisfaction is always in the "now", a timeless glory.

This would be a good time to go back and review our list of questions.

** BOOK MARK **

Reality is timeless. Is it possible for us to be totally free from time and grasp the reality in the timeless to the point that we can always comprehend "what is actually happening". I believe there is only one sure way and that is to "stop" associating with our psychological past. Just stop right now. Stop criticizing, stop condemning, stop scrutinizing and evaluating everything. Remember we are not talking about our chronological past with times and dates but instead it is regarding our negative emotional memories.

You may wonder how do we function, particularly in our every day lives if we are so passive. Many family members and friends with good intentions will try to convince you that it is impossible to function in society especially in the business world and avoid conflict. They will tell you it cannot be done, they will insist that you will only have two choices. One is to hide, quit or separate yourself from the world and the other is to stay and fight.

Many well meaning people can not understand nonresistance or convey that realization through their humanism, the ego can still exist even in an incredibly highly developed spiritual consciousness. They will go so far as to even call you names like weakling or wishy washy. Their arguments will be about good and bad, right and wrong. Just like always society has it backwards.

Instead we are talking about a whole new way of thinking. We must meet our every day affairs in the "new". This is the only way anyone can experience unadulterated success with no power games. We realize that problems are simply new opportunities. Our happiness is not dependent on the outcome based on good or bad, rather we know we have victory already.

There are situations that drastic actions need to take place. In order to be fully present in the "now" you must be free from conflict. If you find yourself in a relationship that you are being mistreated and it is dangerously abusive, by all means take action. This action should not create more suffering to others by you reacting and responding aggressively with a mind of fear and retribution, this would simply be submitting yourself to the ways of death. Instead you need to do one of the following. Leave the situation showing compassion to others recognizing their true beauty behind their abusive actions or make a positive change that will bless and encourage everyone involved.

Part 3
CREATIVE ENERGY

Whenever we think about anything it is always about ourselves which is a result of our memory of past experiences. Is it possible to leave that mentality of "me" which is forever living at a shallow quality of conforming to the ways of the world and move to a so-called deeper level of existence?

What and where is that creative energy that brings about total freedom. This freedom is not the escape that the vain and selfish seek but instead a liberty from the beliefs, traditions and reliance on the customs of society and religion. If we function in the realm of time and memory based on our conditioned mind and at the same time seek eternal happiness we will only manifest duality in our lives and in those around us who we influence and dominate.

To see and understand the whole picture which is an enormous complex movement of life we must watch with awareness from moment to moment. Through this careful watchfulness we create an opportunity to perceive the truth instantly and completely. With a cloudless mind there is no wandering in the dark.

Have you ever been out at sea and a heavy fog moves in? It can be an eerie feeling especially if the vessel is not equipped with instrument technology. Without a depth finder getting to close to the shore could be fatal. A fog horn sounding off at the pier may be the only refuge available to dock safely. This situation happened to me on Lake Michigan on a fishing excursion. The dense fog reduced our visibility to about 50 ft.

We drifted blindly for hours before the fog started to moderately clear and we could to some extent try and find our way back. Periodically we would shut off the motor, be as quiet as possible and listen for the fog horn. I remember straining to listen like I never listened before. As night fall approached I felt our lives could be at jeopardy if we did not find our way back soon. Just as it was getting dark we heard it, that sweet sound of a harbor fog horn. As we followed that sound to safety it became one of my memories that I will never forget.

Listening in silence can often times be the only passage available to entering into that place of refuge where life and reality exist. Can you honestly remember the last time you genuinely listened with total openness? Normally when we think we are giving our full attention to the present moment we are actually giving our consideration through deliberation.

In other words we consider and evaluate the current circumstances through our conditioned intellect and if we agree with it and it fits our theology we welcome it as an addition and enhancement to what we already believe. This is not total uninhibited openness but rather listening through all our past experiences.

I have this good friend that I have known for a long time. This gentleman has proven his honesty to me numerous times. Almost every time we meet we talk about the "word of the day". Not yesterdays significance or tomorrows goals but what the life-force of "today" is revealing to those that have ears to hear and eyes to see. Sometimes he will dare me to consider something out of the ordinary, he will talk about things that I have never considered previously or could even imagine. I have to deliberately tell myself to stop scrutinizing and analyzing what he is sharing with me and simply listen to him with complete sincerity.

To give our undivided attention to any situation can be a great deal more difficult than many of us realize. Sometimes we listen out of resentment as many unhappily married couples do. They appear to be listening by keeping their opinions to themselves however it is only out of bitterness and at the same time they are still judging and condemning on the inside. If we merely listen out of duty we will only feel anger and no one filled with anger can be full of joy, the two cannot mix.

The next time you hear or read someone expressing something extremely contrary to what you believe, mentally stop and give special consideration to your thoughts. If you are not listening with a totally free and open spirit your mind will be secretly condemning and criticizing everything you disagree with. It does not take much effort to hear this inner disapproval because it can be quit forceful at times. I am not going to ask you to start practicing your listening skills because we can only exist in the present moment, instead I will ask you to just do it, now, this instant.

This nonjudgmental and unconditioned attitude energizes a stillness of presence that is absolutely essential in recognizing the certainty in any situation. When our mind is not littered by all the noise of yesterday our thoughts can be empty of all its conditioning, then an eternal creative energy comes into being. In this reality we will find the truth about God.

Part 4
TRUTH REMAINS THE SAME AS IT FOREVER CHANGES

When we seriously desire to experience or obtain something we want, it will usually happen. It is similar when we think we experience truth or God, it is more often than not, simply a projection of our desires, a result of all the influences in the world that we surrender to. For example when we choose a spiritual or political leader, we choose one that will satisfy "our" demands. It's not about seeking truth but rather satisfying "our" desires and goals. It's all about fitting in with "our" bias view points. We always choose a leader that makes us feel safe, agreeing with "our" beliefs. Regrettably if they walk in narrow-mindedness and their life is in turmoil and chaos we will experience the same.

Truth is forever changing, yet at the same time it is never changing. You may ask, how can that be? Let's look at this from the view point of solving a problem. Every problem, no matter what it is, religious, business, political or personal is never the same as before but it is always new and different. The time in history is different, the people are different, the technology is different, the beliefs are different, the location is different, everything is new. So we can never approach a problem with our old conditioning and beliefs.

If we owned a business together and we were looking to hire a business manager we would probably want someone with a lot of experience in the area of our business. Yet if all they possessed was their past experience with no desire to adjust to changing conditions and learn anything new along the way, they would probably be a poor choice. If they settled back lazy and comfortable, and never approached each day with an open mind and fresh energy, they would continue living in yesterday and our business may fail and come to an end.

Sometimes we get hung up on the words and the words themselves become blinders to seeing the whole reality. When race horses are equipped with blinders it is usually to force them to look straight ahead and not be distracted by what is around them as they are driven to win the race. However with humans, the blinders need to be removed in order for us to see the ever changing reality around us. We could call it a spiritual periphery.

Many wild birds and animals peripheral vision is well beyond 250 degrees. This enables them to see and detect danger from almost all directions. Their life often depends on how far in advance they react to a strike from a predator. Their surrounding demands that their awareness is at all times in the now. We can commonly learn countless things from nature.

One set of words that can often confuse people is that "God is the same yesterday, today and forever". We need to understand this with the insight that God/Reality is alive. God is life and life is ever changing, constantly stirring like the wind, forever new. Recently I was visiting a book store promoting one of my books when the manager took a moment and read part of my book. He was only reading for a minute or two when he commented how I must have read a specific book he was familiar with. I stated that I never heard of the book but that I was not surprised by his comments. Truth is universal and all truth originates from the same source. The seeds of illumination exist in all of us.

Truth is never motionless and reality is timeless, as it changes from moment to moment it also remains the same.

If we seek truth with a closed mind, we think we know the absolute truth about almost everything. Reality cannot be restrained in a box such as a closed mind, it is immeasurable, without beginning or end. This is why a religious mind conditioned with self preservation cannot know the truth. When the religious mind believes it knows the complete will of God it has come to the end of seeking truth.

Have you ever had a difficult task outside on a cold and windy day where you needed to wear a lot of clothes? Every movement takes extra energy because of the heavy clothes that weigh you down and resist your actions. It is the same with an old mind, as it builds up layers of complications in our life it becomes more and more a constant struggle to just survive. However as we remove all the layers of the old consciousness we feel light and energetic, liberated from our daily anxiety, stress and worries. We feel just like a kid without a care in the world.

As you continue to read this book I would like to again remind you to look past the words and see what the meaning of the statement is speaking to you. This may seem strange that I ask you to read a book full of words and then to look past those words. Sometimes our trained thinking can get hung up on terminology especially if we are well read on certain ideals such as religion and politics. For example the word "hope" can be used in many ways. Religion uses the word "hope" as a stepping stone to a future paradise, conversely in this book we use the word "hope" as something that keeps us harmfully focused on the future and prevents us from living in the eternal present.

Another example are the words "overcome the world". Society's definition of overcoming is to conquer and dominate anything and everything that prevents you from obtaining what you desire. In contrast, in these writings we recognize that nothing "real" can be in jeopardy or lost. We respect everything but only the artificial things like names and shapes pass away. So again I ask you the reader to proceed with an open mind.

Part 5
TO BE CREATIVE IS TO BE FREE FROM THE PAST

Humans seek happiness in this world of disorder so we choose paths that are more convenient to satisfy our selfish goals. We choose a course of action which assures us of a reward. We even create a God that is based on our desires for happiness. We think of God through all our past knowledge. The problem is that we live our whole life based on the past which is of time and then we try to experience the timeless.

In time we continually want to change the where, what and when, but even if we are trying to change it for the good it is still destructive because we want to be something that we are not. As long as we are happy, we want everything to stay the same but the problem arises when things in our life cause us sorrow, then we go to great lengths to change it.

We get scared if we don't get our way. When we get scared we try to impose our beliefs upon ourselves and others. Then what happens, our mind becomes crowded with anger and we become hard, incapable of being sensitive, open and flexible.

** BOOK MARK **

Throughout history we have been taught that if we do certain things or perform a certain way, the end result will be that we will find favor with God. God is not a commodity that we can trade or sell in the market place.

Many humans are conditioned by external influences such as religious dogma and social pressures. It has become extremely difficult to think with a clear and creative mind due to our inward hunger to succeed at or improve something. Can we simply rest in the knowledge that the past is forever gone and the future is not here yet. We will never realize the immeasurable when we discipline our actions with a goal for the future.

Life is now, living from moment to moment. So to be totally creative is to be free from the past, free from what others have experienced and told us. Instead we need a quiet spirit to understand the timeless. When we accept and submit to "what is" our past no longer has control over us.

It becomes very difficult to be creative in our thinking if we are cultured and influenced by political and religious doctrine, by our beliefs, and by our own selfish desires to achieve something or change something. Self-discipline is still conformity to a belief that you need to change in the future. We discipline ourselves and try to conform to religious leaders or to what society believes because we feel if we imitate those who appear to be happy, wise and rich, we to will be happy.

Have you ever noticed what happens when we try to change or improve ourselves to become something different and then we fail or stumble in our endeavor to do so? Misery, despair and frustration always follow because self improvement is all about "me". Then because we are sad we feel our forms of escape such as our God, our movies, our activities become imperative to survive. Unfortunately the many forms of escape we choose are only a one-way street to suffering and chaos. Subsequently we become negative and condemn everyone around us because we have set up an artificial set of standards due to our self-centeredness.

The next time you hear someone tell you that you must stop sinning or you must stop doing this or that, or you must start doing something, ask yourself what is their purpose or goal. It is frequently about saving themselves (the old man) or forcing the old man to change into something else to gain something. Life is not about overcoming anything, instead it is obtaining immortality by living in the "now", it is "thinking" outside the old conditioned mind and it is leaving behind "self" with all its fears and escapes.

Let's look at this a little closer. For example, why is it that most younger automobile drivers drive faster than those who are older. Younger drivers are simply not 'aware" or informed of many of the dangers on today's highways. It's more than gaining time behind the wheel, the younger drivers in fact have better eye sight and better reactions than many of the older drivers. We can try to force them to slow down, we can punish them and they still drive fast.

Nonetheless, have you ever noticed a young couple when they start to raise a family with small children of their own, they very seldom drive fast past a playground full of kids playing or speed down a road when kids are playing in the street. They become aware of what is happening around them. The old mind can't be disciplined to obey but instead reality of the moment sets all of us free to live safely.

Awareness is different than legalism, we can only find truth when we stop escaping. Observation without condemnation brings understanding because genuine awareness is the end of "self", it is the liberation from the old man and the freedom from our old thoughts. Then living in the "now" becomes a reality.

Living in the "now" is particularly challenging because it requires us to be exceptionally open, sensitive and workable. In exchange however, those of you who live in the "now" are not weighted down with the cares of the world but are as light as a feather, full of positive energy, flowing freely where the spirit/wind blows. You are never old because you have no beginning or end.

I would like to take a moment and have you look with me at a subtlety that is difficult to explain. I will do my best to convey my thoughts and hopefully you will grasp the elusive distinction between good and that which goes beyond good. Nearly all religions teach about good and bad, right and wrong, holy and evil. Yet everyone's view about what is good and what is bad can be worlds apart.

We expect to perceive things differently with those who live on the opposite side of the world but even our own family members can judge and conclude many things contrary to how we see them. This can become a problem in a close relationships if anyone in the union tries to live a blameless life by following a standard of good and bad, right and wrong.

At first this life of "doing good" appears noble and beneficial, nevertheless the purpose for legalistic deeds of righteousness are forever manifested from the belief of reward and punishment. The basis is always selfishness, to earn a reward for 'me", to receive a prize for "me" or to avoid a penalty.

Those who evaluate their lives founded on the conviction of good or bad, who constantly judge and condemn cannot comprehend freedom. They will constantly be trying to convince others especially their loved ones about the evil they observe. They will not rest until everyone around them sees and reacts to the wickedness that they are so sure is real. Their life of legalism and judging themselves and everyone else will sooner or later become to much to endure. Hopefully they will come to the end of themselves soon for their sake and for the sake of anyone they influence.

Here comes the delicate part. If you have a loved one who has problems when you interpret good and bad differently than they do, they will go totally wacky if you don't judge or condemn at all. When you don't require anything, not an answer, not a solution, they will accuse you of indulging in the evil they perceive. The fear they feel will become overwhelming, they will not want to be around you.

Can you see the slight variation here. There is no indulgence in evil, there is only awareness to everything around you. If you ever want to be a blessing to your neighbor and minister life to those in need, this is the only way possible, with a spirit of understanding and acceptance, not judging or condemning anyone or anything.

Part 6
YOU AND I MAKE UP SOCIETY

Society is a result of everyone's relationship to each other including you and I. Our innermost nature constantly influences our outward circumstances. Maybe this is why we are told to pray for our enemies. This prayer for others may also be a prayer for ourselves. Sometimes we can be our own worst enemy. If we ourselves and our so called enemies walk with an enlightened awareness, then complete unity will follow.

Do you understand how showing compassion to our enemies removes the conflict in our lives. Conflict is a result of "our" everyday life. War is the outer manifestation of "our" inward struggle. We are the cause of war because of our religious, political or economical beliefs. These beliefs breed fear causing a desire for control, status, prestige, wealth, nationalism and the desire for organized religion, worshiping a doctrine. We talk about peace but secretly we are induced by greed.

When we stop thinking about ourselves and care enough about others to pray for them, we communion without fear, free to understand each other. When we put others first, our relationships are not built on self perpetuation and self protection. When we don't put others first we seek security through our relationships and if these relationships do not satisfy us we get scared and uncertain about our future. This uncertainty causes us to become envious, aggressive, possessive, condemning, demanding protection. We then seek that protection behind walls that we call duty and responsibility because we know not how to love.

All over the world there are wealthy (worldly wealth) business owners who have many employees working for them. Some of them feel that they are very powerful and "wield a mighty sword". They only appreciate those that can benefit them. When someone mistreats them or does something that they disagree with, they remember it for a long time. Most of us have heard the cliché "don't get mad just get even". Due to their ambition and aggression these business men and women make many enemies along the way. They often keep a carefully protected memory bank of everyone they want to retaliate at some day.

We have it backwards if we want to harm those who we think is our enemy. This myopic attitude will only lead to self destruction. To have peace we must be peaceful. To put an end to the external hostilities we must stop the battles inside ourselves. Peace is more than an idea, it is not simply about me or you, it is about the entire harmony with complete communion, not aimed at one or two, but communion with the highest.

Part 7
TAKE A BREAK AND REST

Do you ever feel like you just need a time out away from all the turmoil around you. Let's change directions for a short time and examine the social pressures we encounter in our everyday lives. Have you ever been given a hard time by your friends, classmates or co-workers for doing what's right, for refusing to go along with the crowd because you know it is wrong. Yesterday I was called a coward because I refused to partake in a business dispute.

Most of us have been taught to be strong and stand up for our rights to the point of tearing down those around us. It would be an insult to be called a coward and we should fight to prove we have courage. Let us look at this more closely. When we are accused of not fighting for our rights, the accusations always come from others who are afraid and are responding out of fear. The criticism is based on someone wanting to change something.

** BOOK MARK **

Our conditioned reasoning receives condemnation as a insult but if it is based on our actions of nonresistance we should take it as an indication that we are not resisting "what is" and are living in the present moment.

In the United States, in the state of Florida, there is a common saying that goes like this, "we can get rid of the alligators but what about the pigs". The residents of Florida are finding out that as the alligator population is declining due to human development, the native pig population is increasing dramatically. The pigs natural predator is the alligator. Each time we change something there must be a corresponding reaction. It is the same when we react negatively toward criticism we become the pig, rooting around in other peoples garbage.

This process of trying to protect ourselves can be extremely tiresome. However it does not have to be like that, as we live in the "now" we will understanding that what others say and how they act really has nothing to do with us but it is about their fears and their desires to change something. Therefore we can relax and enjoy life at home, at work or at school with a positive energy that will encourage everyone around us, even if they are critical and demanding.

I am frequently challenged concerning the need to fight for the rights of minorities and those who are weak and vulnerable. I am not advocating that any of us should forget or neglect those in need. Many people of wisdom and books of enlightenment remind us to give to those in need, help the down trodden, and remember to visit the widow and those in prison. However we need to remember that when we resist evil and fight against it and pray against it we only give it power.

Sometimes our own actions give the evil permission to exist in our lives and the lives of our loved ones. In reality evil has no power, it can only function through fear, the fear in its own beliefs to change something and the fear it tries to force upon its victims.

Are you beginning to see how fear can be a relentless companion to those who look at life through the eyes of the past. Life becomes a hostile environment, a continuous struggle of power games resulting with the feeling that everyone is out to get you. Even if we take a day off from work or go on a vacation the negative noise never stops.

How do we turn off the power button, how do we destroy the negative energy field (our ego) and get rid of fear.

First we need to fully understand that we need not conquer fear. If we don't completely recognize how fear works we will unconsciously try to defeat it over and over again which will only result in added tension. We end up like a rodent trapped in a cage, we go around and around never going anywhere.

It is our old consciousness that is still deep-seated within that creates fear. This is why it is so important to grasp how our old mind functions in order to bring an end to fear. Most of our endeavors are escapes from "what is happening right now" and we become exhausted and worn out. Instead of fighting "what is" simply take a rest, be quiet. When we are quiet we are not afraid. When we are still reality is discovered.

Wholeness influences and stimulates every aspect of our being. All around us are people who disregard the well being of the environment. If we watch and listen intently we will understand why they close their eyes and ignore the welfare of this beautiful planet we all share and live on. The more any of us ignores the health of our plant reveals the degree of self-centeredness we our trapped in. Those who have the most to gain financially are usually those that care the least.

As our awareness is heightened our concern regarding environment pollution, pesticides and poisons will intensify, and we will live a healthier, safer life style. We will grow and eat more organic whole foods which results in a healthier body and a safer environment for all of Gods creatures.

Our appreciation for the physical world is the result of our admiration for society as a whole. Enlightened human beings spontaneously restore and sustain the health of themselves and everyone and everything around them. With a healthier being we are often more active helping others in need. We aren't spending all our time and energy caring for ourselves and the many sicknesses that plague a life style of gluttony, greed, resentment, condemnation and anger.

In Proverbs it states that a merry heart is like a medicine. It is a well known fact that people who are loving, compassionate, full of peace and joy are much more healthy than those who are not. Even though eating healthy is important, it is our inner immune system that matters the most. We can take all the vitamins we want, we can eat organic foods and practice all the physical cleansing applications available, we can exercise until we are blue in the face, but if our inner being is not at peace, our outer body will not be complete, whole and healthy.

Forever captivated in our past negative memories and our worries about the future can be a curse to our physical well being. Always judging and condemning circumstances and other peoples actions is a disease. When we judge others and call them names we are actually identifying who and what we are, scared, angry and self-absorbed. This dysfunctional spiritual illness can eat away and diminish every aspect of our radiant being. Negative energy weakens us and is simply bad for the health of our total being.

For fast acting relief, try slowing down. So take a break from all the guilt and bitterness from your past, from all the worry and anxiety about tomorrow and enjoy the present. Stop chasing after your fears, instead the next time you get the chance to sing or dance, do it, celebrate your good fortune that you and the almighty are one. Have some fun, this is what we are all created to do, dance the dance of life for it is enjoyable, exciting and full of healing and redemption.

Positive energy is like an anti-depressant with no harmful side affects, it not only heals your spirit, soul and body, it purifies everyone near you. Let your true beauty and divinity radiate out to everyone around you with a huge smile and with words and deeds of support. You can only give away what you possess so let it be love, peace and compassion. See the true beauty in everything and everyone.

Part 8
WHAT ABOUT GOD

It is amazing how the human ego attaches itself to anything that will protect and reinforce it's own beliefs. You may wonder why I would start writing a chapter regarding God by addressing the human ego. Many of our beliefs in God are based on our self projected ideas we created over time or were taught by others in order to escape our fears. Then we mutually unite to defend our beliefs because we feel safe when we have others around us not threatening our foundations that we have spent our whole life building. This collective personality can be extremely destructive to itself and society.

What is God? Who is God? Can we know and comprehend something that is beyond measure, something that is eternal, which really does not mean unlimited time but rather that time does not exist in the realm of life. Can we measure the immeasurable, can we describe the indescribable? We must be free of time, free from all ideas about God. If we take an honest look at what nearly everyone believes or thinks about God, we will see that their belief system always reaches back to which religion they grew up with and what part of the world they grew up in. Even if we try to run away from our traditional background and strive and study to be free of our past religious training, our existing and past culture continues to pollute our minds. We generally comprehend and interpret based on what others have told us.

Time is a significant barrier stopping us from knowing God. When our minds are trapped in the memories of days gone by or consumed with the worries of tomorrow, we are held hostage with our eyes covered and blind folded with fear. This shroud of time traps us in a place where suffering can exist. Religion enforces the belief that the highest reward possible we can obtain is in the future. It reinforces the conviction that the present moment is never acceptable and the future will be better. We constantly fret about what may happen to us in the future. We waste our whole life waiting for God to do something.

God illumination is revealed when we enter a dwelling place of wholeness which can only be occupied in the now. As we honor the present reality we are noiseless and therefore free from our past memories projecting their own desires. Then our entire peaceful being can experience the existence of the ageless. The eternal is revealed from moment to moment and only when our mind and spirit is not overtaken with thoughts of self. If we want to know something that is outside of time, if we want to experience the eternal source, the God essence, we will need to come into that presence with a totally free spirit.

God, truth and reality are alive, forever new. However all of our knowledge and all our religious practices are the opposite, they are the products of memory which is old. The spirit of God is never old it is always new and if we are capable of approaching reality in the present, in the now, the fruits of the spirit will surely follow. God's indwelling divinity will be awakened in each of us and we will become an undividable part of this timeless nature.

What does all that actually mean? The realm of God is within each of us. To know God and His eternal presence is to die to oneself. The path that leads to reality is narrow and few are those that find it. Consider yourself very fortunate if you can dwell in that most holy place where your selfish striving ceases and the joy of His Being flows through you. Truth, reality or God, what ever you want to call it, is alive and can only survive in a house that is free, pure and alive. Each of us are that holy, living place where God takes up residence. When we love there is no need to search for God because God is love. Rejoice, we are all created in Gods image. Be glad, ye are holy as He is holy.

Part 9
PRAYER

There are countless books written about prayer. Every religion and every society provides us with a clever procedure to follow that promises us success with our prayer requests. Are you willing to examine this question about prayer honestly and with an open spirit? If you are we will see that most instructions related to prayer are all about "I, me and self".

Have you ever been lost and you stopped and ask someone for directions? Now just imagine the person you are asking directions from is not familiar with the area and they're not even sure of their immediate location. It would be impossible to acquire accurate directions from someone who does not even know where they are. Both of you are kind of lost. This could be compared to many who tell us how to pray and what to pray for.

A few paragraphs earlier I referred to God revealing Himself through us which results in the fruits of His spirit manifesting in our lives. These God qualities such as Love, Peace, Joy, Compassion, Patience and Faith are great indicators that reveal the presence of reality in our life and the lives of those around us. These God qualities are present because "I, me and self" are not. In the book of James he tells us that our prayers are not answered because we ask amiss.

When we pray we are normally in search of a reward that will satisfy our desires. Repeatedly it's about fixing all the problems we created. Our prayers remain powerless as long as we continue to exist in self-centeredness. A person who prays out of selfishness has no love or concern for others because a self-seeking prayer is all about oneself, obtaining things like self protection and self advancement.

The carnal mind secretly doesn't want to be free of its troubles, it thrives on them, it receives its identity from them. Some of you may say, that's not true, many of my prayers are answered. Even though many of us receive when we ask, what we receive is not reality. Don't be mistaken that when your prayer is answered that you are one with God. If we remain small-minded, greedy and ambitious the inner voice we hear is frequently our own voice forecasting our self-absorbed goals.

** BOOK MARK **

Evil has no power, consequently the only thing it can do is to deceive the weak in spirit into believing that it does. It works similar to a nation with a military spreading propaganda about how great its armed forces are. The weaker they are the more lies and propaganda they need to spread to try and fool those who are stronger than they are.

In reality there is only one power, not two, but deep down we will not accept that there is only one power. Most people will agree that there is only one all powerful, all present, all knowing, all good force in the universe but then everything they confess and pray about proclaims the opposite.

When we pray we are simply spreading and reinforcing the lies regarding the strength of the illusion. We resist the lie, we give it power in our lives, we verbally declare its power before everyone, we submit to it, we believe in it and then we force it on those we influence. This is why the existence of the fruits of the spirit in our lives are good indicators revealing the reality about our petitions.

Nonresistance is in fact faith, we see the reality when others see the illusion and believe the lie. The eyes of faith can clearly see that all things that are real are as they are suppose to be and there is no need to fight the deception and defend our personal finite point of view. Patience then becomes strength knowing all things have their place and time.

We've all heard the phase "turn the other cheek". This act of awareness can be tremendously demanding when we are running short on patience. Driving our car in stop and go traffic can test the best of us especially when we feel we need to be somewhere important and the traffic delays will cause us to be late. Road rage is about people lashing out at others because they feel slower traffic or drivers that butt ahead of them are preventing them from achieving their goals. We mistakenly believe that we are a victim and our time is being stolen from us. Then we get mad and retaliate. An even bigger problem occurs when other drivers feel the same anger towards us. When egos clash, things get "out of control".

By resisting "the present moment" we are making others our enemy and we contaminate the spirit of peace because of our resentment. Sometimes this contamination takes place on the way to a family gathering or on the road to a place of worship and prayer. We don't realize how extremely contagious our spirit of aggression and self righteous hostility can be. We could call this condition sanctimonious OCD with poor awareness.

What is OCD, Obsessive Compulsive Disorder? The foundation for OCD says it is a medical brain disorder that causes problems in processing information. The brain gets stuck on a particular thought or urge and just cannot let go. A mental hiccup that won't go away. To break it down even further, obsessions are thoughts, images or impulses that occur over and over again and feel "out of control". The obsessions are accompanied by feelings of fear, disgust, worries and doubt. The compulsion is typically trying to make the obsessions (fears) go away by performing acts over and over again.

OCD symptoms cause distress and embezzle a lot of time and energy. When someone with OCD does not recognize that their beliefs and actions are unreasonable, this is called OCD with poor insight. This physical condition of OCD can be compared to our spiritual obsessions where we feel "scared and out of control" hoping and suffering that our prayers will be answered to our liking. Also similar is our compulsions of requesting over and over and over, hoping that the answer to our prayers will make our fears go away.

A human spirit that is praying, supplicating, demanding, begging, pleading, confused and lost cannot understand the whole picture, the whole reality. We can narrowly understand the truth of the matter when our mind and spirit is unconditionally still, not desiring and insisting anything. When we enter our prayer closet with a totally still heart and mind with no desires, not even for good, then we can experience the will of God.

Are you really serious and willing to completely give up your egotistical desires because that is a requirement to have the faith to move mountains. A man who has relinquished his selfish goals is fully alive, he knows that he is the living temple of God/Reality and does not pray the "I, me, self" prayer because he does NOT desire anything. After our mind and spirit are entirely silent and still, that which is eternal comes into being.

A short time ago a young gentleman asked me why we should want to see outside the box, see outside our conditioned thinking. He said he didn't want to know anything about the suffering in the world, he likes living in his comfortable little corner of the world. This desire to remain detached and protected is blindness in itself. When people have eye surgery and have their cataracts removed, they regularly comment that they never knew what they were missing. It is the same with a petty and vain mind, it does not even know what is beyond itself. To go beyond our self-seeking goals is the purpose of life, the purpose of our existence, our true essence.

As the cataracts of our old consciousness are removed, we will recognize our true identity and everyone else's true reality behind their actions of sanctimonious OCD, As we yield to the flow of life instead of resisting it, our gentle spirit will magnetize and bless everyone around us.

When we show tolerance to others they learn to be patient.
When we accept others they feel loved.
When we show approval to others they like themselves.
When we are honest others can also be truthful.
When we live with security others will have faith in themselves & others.
When we honor others they learn to appreciate.
When we encourage others they feel confident.
When we are compassionate to others they learn the world is a beautiful place in which to live.

It has been written that the most important attributes are faith, hope and love, and love being the most important of all. Through love everything flows. Where there is love there is life, where there is love there is truth, where there is love there is reality, where there is love there is God. This is the excellence that has no opposite, this is the good that has no bad, this is the joy that has no sadness, this is the peace that has no fear, this is the faith that the miracle of life on this earth is all about.

When my older children were still in middle school our family spent many evenings sitting around a camp fire in our backyard. We would often invite our friends and neighbors to come and join us around the fire. One night we were talking about our true identity and since we are all part of the same collective body, the children of God, created in His image, we were all going to change our last name to "Christ". The word Christ can be defined as the "anointed" or "the divine manifestation of God, in the flesh to destroy incarnate error".

We started calling each other by our first name and then added "Christ" for our last name. For example Julie was now Julie Christ and Andy was now Andy Christ. The kids then shortened it up and called everyone by their initials, so Andy Christ was now AC, and Julie Christ was now JC. A few weeks later we gathered around the campfire again. This time we were talking about since we all are "anointed" that we were going to drop our first names and everyone would simple go by the same name "Christ". Andy didn't like this idea because he wanted to keep his new nick name, AC. Andy's innocent wish of not wanting to give up his new nick name illustrates how humans resist the idea of dropping their identity.

We struggle and fight and do everything we can to prevent our old identity from passing away. We name churches and businesses after ourselves. We construct buildings and monuments to glorify our old man. We openly give many things to charity hoping everyone will take notice. Our actions of self glorification are always about gaining something we believe we need in order to continue. In reality though, the death of the old man is disposing of everything that is not the real you. The amazing mystery of life is revealed when we let the old man, the old consciousness, die prior to our physical, earthly body passing away. We then discover that there is no death. Once the old man is no more, your true being is revealed.

In several holy writings we are instructed to stop praying until we forgive those that have mistreated us. Can we forgive ourselves or others if we continue to dwell on the past or walk in self absorption? People who repeatedly get emotionally hurt can never accept "what is". Their response is not action but instead it is a reaction due to their fears based on an illusion. They take everything personal and feel everything is about themselves. The whole structure of forgiveness is the opposite, how can anyone be ill-treated or harmed in any way when we are created in Gods image, indestructible and immortal. Forgiveness becomes nonexistent the moment our old nature is left behind.

Part 10
RELATIONSHIPS

There are many different kind of relationships, for example the bond we have with our pets, the relationship we have with our family and friends, the association we have with our classmates, co-workers and our boss, the conflict with someone who can hurt us or our loved ones, the fear we feel towards somebody or something that presents a threat to us. And we can not forget about those relationships that seem to be the most difficult, those who has victimized us and we cannot forgive.

There are many key elements to any functional or dysfunctional relationship. We classify our relationships as good or bad, we subconsciously assign them levels of importance based on what we can achieve or lose through them. Unfortunately most relationships are based on selfishness, what one party can obtain from the other. We look for mutual goals and try to build from there. When our goals are not being fulfilled we then feel there is no benefit to continue the relationship and we end it.

Every relationship we are involved in we give a different level of value. Let's take for example our colleagues, co-workers show less respect to those below them on the corporate ladder than they do to those above them who could possible in the future help or influence their chances of getting promoted or receiving a salary increase. Again not living in the present moment.

We can even see this intolerance in the church system, pastors will often times show favoritism to those who give large amount of money to their house of worship or to those who hold political positions that may help further their cause someday. This is probably why we are instructed to tithe in secret, otherwise our benevolence is really a personal advertisement to glorify ourselves.

We have all heard stories about the good Samaritan who stopped and helped a person along the road that was beaten and robbed. Everyone else passed by and looked the other way. Why did the others not stop and help someone in need, because they had nothing to gain. Sales people find themselves in a unique profession, their time, energy and money is reserved stringently for those that they have something to gain from. It is impossible to understand our own existence if we are using our relationships to achieve and further our goals.

Can you remember a personal relationship from your past which you are no longer closely involved in and you were the one by and large responsible for the termination. The other person or persons were generally satisfied with what they were receiving out of their association with you yet you were in dire need to receive more comfort or less pain.

A pure unadulterated relationship is not about what we can receive but instead what we can give. We are not talking about becoming a martyr sacrificing ourselves for the greedy desires of the other, instead love is recognizing that everyone is part of the whole. Most of the problems we experience in our relationships are due to our own desires resulting out of our own fears. We remain in a relationship only if it fulfills us, pleases us and we feel secure.

In order for any union between two or more people to survive and flourish we must first understand ourselves, why and how we respond to everything. Anthony Quale once said "To understand a man, you must know his memories". I would like to change that a little, to understand ourselves we must know our own memories and how and why we respond to them. Everything we do is a reaction originating out of our past experiences.

Finally, our relationships will only succeed when we place others ahead of ourselves. We are able to put others first when we realize that we are not depended on anyone to fulfill our needs. Compassion is perceiving the inherent bond between yourself and all living things. We impart age lasting life to others with the understanding that each and everyone of us are an intricate part of the "whole", full of vitality and power. This power is not the domination and aggression society tries to inflict on others due to its fear instead it is the power and ability to love and encourage everyone you come in contact with.

CONCLUSION

Remember the ** BOOK MARK ** in chapter one where we could go back and reference questions when we experience the mistaken feeling that we are lacking something. The majority of the time when we believe we need or want something is based on comparing it to what others have or don't have.

Let us look at this issue of comparison one more time. Imagine that you were driving on a busy freeway. You are in the express lane traveling substantially less than the speed limit yet the vehicles in all the other lanes are moving at a much slow rate than you. Even though you wish you could drive a little faster the feeling of passing everyone next to you makes you feel superior.

Now let's change this slightly and you are traveling at or even above the posted speed limit however all the traffic in the adjoining lanes are passing you. You feel anxious, you desperately want to speed up and go as fast as everyone else. You are already driving the speed limit or faster but that's not good enough. Their actions in correlation to yours influences you to the point that it destroys your tranquility. Stress is the unequivocal result associated with constantly wanting, desiring or not accepting what is.

If you are earnest and sincere about experiencing total freedom immediately and continuously, comparison needs to have no part of your life. This place of non-comparison is a secret dwelling where nothing can influence you and your spirit overflows with the attitude of "thanksgiving". Illumination is not just about knowing the truth it is about "being" the truth. The harmony and quality of being that many seekers are searching for is not some day in the future, rather it is at this moment.

I would like you to try a little experiment. Stand face to face with someone you feel comfortable with, then both of you reach out your hands and push against each others hands. Have the other person start out pushing lightly and then increase the pressure. You will notice the greater the other person pushes towards you the greater you need to resist in order to hold your position. Now try the opposite, when they push towards you, you don't push back. This nonresistance may seem like you are allowing the other person to achieve what they want and in doing so affect you. Not so.

In many ways the outer resistance we experience in our everyday lives is simply in our minds. The more intently we resist the flow of life, the greater emotional stress that it produces. Allow your inner wall of resistance to fade away, offer no opposition to the ignorance of society, otherwise you'll just attempt to defend your insecurities and get injured. Instead take every situation that appears negative and expose its true identity for what it really is, a positive movement of life. Let the fierce winds that rage all around us glide through you as if you are a giant wind mill. The faster and stronger the lies of the ego driven world blow, the more life energy you produce and share with those in need.

Our 'self-esteem man" believes as we obtain spiritual understanding we should become popular. Everyone around us will notice our great awareness, our wonderful insight, our powerful faith and our gracious benevolence. This again is the desire to be accepted and well liked by others due to our fears. Can you recognize that these goals of popularity and fame prove the old selfish nature still exist. If we desire to have our name up in lights or on the front cover of a magazine we are right back where we started from, living in fear, hoping to save our old man.

If we feel that we are something exceptional, above the ordinary, we have missed the mark. In this day and age many of the larger religious organizations are starting to break apart and meet in smaller groups at home meetings. If these groups simply meet to sit among others that agree with their beliefs and talk about how wonderfully enlightened they all are, then enlightenment has not taken place.

Illumination is overflowing with the fruits of the spirit such as humility and compassion. Everyone who is truly blessed with the gifts of faith and love are always full of joy, the joy that is not dependent on outward circumstances. Thanksgiving is interwoven in every aspect of their being. Their acts and deeds of love almost always occur unnoticed. There are no proclamations broadcasting their kindness and generosity. They aren't known by their outward and superficial acts of good deeds, humility doesn't brag about itself. Most truly spiritual people are never noticed except by other selfless awakened beings.

Don't be fooled by the trickery and lies of the popular religious and social systems proclaiming their greatness, instead true awareness claims no one, authentic illumination identifies nobody, real revelation glorifies none, genuine enlightenment takes us beyond ourselves.

As we go beyond "self", compassion and thanksgiving spontaneously come into existence. In contrast it is virtually impossible to genuinely feel thankful and caring if we are seeking to satisfy "me". For example when we label other people with shameful and degrading names it is a sure sign that our intentions are not pure and we are not placing others ahead of ourselves but instead it brings to light that we are more concerned about our selfish desires then the well being of the whole. We ignorantly deny that we are one with each other and the source of all things. This illusion of separateness which creates duality in our life must be done away with.

The understanding concerning love and oneness is the final hurdle that many so called spiritually enlightened people sadly cannot rise above. Truth scares them and jeopardizes their "sense of self man" who wants to stay a separate and special entity, otherwise it cannot remain in power. When we come into the ultimate truth, love will manifest in our lives with the understanding that no one is separate instead everyone is part of our own being. When we love others we love our self. There is no other.

In the quietness and gentleness of love your spirit will rise to the divinity that your identity is no more.

Go in peace with the understanding that life after death is not some other place and time, it is now.

978-0-595-38464-8
0-595-38464-1

Printed in the United States
45142LVS00002B/25-27